HIP-HOP

Alicia Keys
Ashanti
Beyoncé
Black Eyed Peas
Busta Rhymes
Chris Brown
Christina Aguilera
Ciara
Cypress Hill
Daddy Yankee
DMX
Don Omar
Dr. Dre
Eminem
Fat Joe
50 Cent
The Game
Hip-Hop: A Short History
Hip-Hop Around the World
Ice Cube
Ivy Queen
Jay-Z
Jennifer Lopez
Juelz Santana
Kanye West

Lil Wayne
LL Cool J
Lloyd Banks
Ludacris
Mariah Carey
Mary J. Blige
Missy Elliot
Nas
Nelly
Notorious B.I.G.
OutKast
Pharrell Williams
Pitbull
Queen Latifah
Reverend Run (of Run DMC)
Sean "Diddy" Combs
Snoop Dogg
T.I.
Tupac
Usher
Will Smith
Wu-Tang Clan
Xzibit
Young Jeezy
Yung Joc

She dreamed of becoming a big star from the time she was very young. Ciara has realized her dream!

Ciara

Jacquelyn Simone

Mason Crest Publishers

Ciara

Produced by Harding House Publishing Service, Inc., 201 Harding Avenue, Vestal, NY 13850.

MASON CREST PUBLISHERS INC.
370 Reed Road
Broomall, Pennsylvania 19008
(866)MCP-BOOK (toll free)
www.masoncrest.com

Printed in the United States of America

13 12 11 10 09   10 9 8 7 6 5 4 3 2

Library of Congress Cataloging-in-Publication Data

Simone, Jacquelyn.
  Ciara / Jacquelyn Simone.
    p. cm. — (Hip-hop)
  Includes bibliographical references and index.
  ISBN 978-1-4222-0286-9
  ISBN: 978-1-4222-0077-3 (series)
  1. Ciara (Vocalist)—Juvenile literature. 2. Singers—United States—Biography—Juvenile literature. I. Title.
ML3930.C47S56 2008
782.42164092—dc22
[B]
                    2007031165

Publisher's notes:
• All quotations in this book come from original sources and contain the spelling and grammatical inconsistencies of the original text.

• The Web sites mentioned in this book were active at the time of publication. The publisher is not responsible for Web sites that have changed their addresses or discontinued operation since the date of publication. The publisher will review and update the Web site addresses each time the book is reprinted.

DISCLAIMER: The following story has been thoroughly researched, and to the best of our knowledge, represents a true story. While every possible effort has been made to ensure accuracy, the publisher will not assume liability for damages caused by inaccuracies in the data, and makes no warranty on the accuracy of the information contained herein. This story has not been authorized nor endorsed by Ciara.

Contents

Hip-Hop Time Line

1976 Grandmaster Flash and the Furious Five emerge as one of the first battlers and freestylers.

1984 The track "Roxanne Roxanne" sparks the first diss war.

1970s DJ Kool Herc pioneers the use of breaks, isolations, and repeats using two turn-tables.

1988 Hip-hop record sales reach 100 million annually.

1982 Afrika Bambaataa tours Europe in another hip-hop first.

1970s Grafitti artist Vic begins tagging on New York subways.

1980 Rapper Kurtis Blow sells a million records and makes the first nationwide TV appearance for a hip-hop artist.

1985 The film *Krush Groove*, about the rise of Def Jam Records, is released.

1970

1980

1970s The central elements of the hip-hop culture begin to emerge in the Bronx, New York City.

1983 Ice-T releases his first singles, marking the earliest examples of gangsta rap.

1986 Run DMC cover Aerosmith's "Walk this Way" and appear on the cover of *Rolling Stone*.

1979 "Rapper's Delight," by The Sugarhill Gang, goes gold.

1984 *Graffitti Rock*, the first hip-hop television program, premieres.

1974 Afrika Bambaataa organizes the Universal Zulu Nation.

1981 Grandmaster Flash and the Furious Five release *Adventures on the Wheels of Steel*.

1988 MTV premieres *Yo! MTV Raps*.

1989 *Billboard* recognizes rap music as a category.

1993 Snoop Dogg's debut album *Doggystyle* becomes the first hip-hop album to debut at #1.

2003 50 Cent debuts with *Get Rich or Die Tryin.*

2006 The Smithsonian National Museum of American History announces the creation of a new hip-hop exhibition, scheduled to open in two years.

1997 The Notorious B.I.G. is gunned down in Los Angeles.

1990s Hip-hop gains popularity in Europe.

2007 Grandmaster Flash and the Furious Five are the first rap artists to be inducted into the Rock and Roll Hall of Fame.

1994 Nas releases *Illmatic*, which becomes the first album to ever receive a five out of five rating from *The Source*.

2004 The first National Hip-Hop Political Convention is held in New Jersey.

1990

2000

1994 In Puerto Rico, the musical genre that had been called "Dem Bow" or "Underground" now starts to be referred to as "Reggaeton."

2004 Daddy Yankee's single "Gasolina" rockets into mainstream popularity in the US, marking the rise of reggaeton in the US.

1990 In Puerto Rico, DJs inspired by Panamanian reggae begin to produce their own music.

1996 Tupac Shakur is killed in Las Vegas.

2003 For the first time, the top ten artists on the *Billboard* charts are all African American. Notably, they are all part of the Dirty South.

1992 DJ Playero releases his mixtape *32*, which has some of the earliest examples of reggaeton recorded, including a track by Daddy Yankee.

2001 Russell Simmons founds the Hip-hop Action Network.

2007 Numerous hip-hop artists perform at the Live Earth concerts, which take place around the globe.

Many consider the Grammy Awards to be the ultimate honor in music. Some artists go their entire careers without even receiving a nomination, let alone a statue. Ciara was amazed when she was nominated for four—and took home one—after fewer than two years as a pro.

1

The First Lady of Crunk & B

The flashing of cameras illuminated a green carpet and numerous stars. The setting sun shone over the Staples Center in Los Angeles as the crowd brimmed with anticipation. The 48th Annual Grammy Awards were about to begin.

From the throng of photographers and celebrities emerged a young woman in a white chiffon dress. Her accessories and rhinestone belt made her shimmer with every step, and her raven hair was pulled back in a ponytail. Ciara had arrived at the Grammys.

This day, February 8, 2006, would bring one of the most monumental honors in the budding star's career. Even though she had been on the popular music scene for less than two years, she had been nominated for four Grammy Awards. She went to the prestigious awards ceremony with the possibility of winning honors for Best New Artist, Best Rap/Sung Collaboration for "1, 2 Step" (with rapper Missy Elliott), Best Rap Song, and Best

Short Form Music Video (both for Missy Elliott's "Lose Control," on which she had been featured). She was shocked to even be considered: she told *Rolling Stone* that, on the day the nominations were announced, "I looked at my pager, and one of my old friends e-mailed me and said, 'Congratulations on your nomination.' And I was like, 'Huh? What nomination?' Then it said, 'Grammy.'"

At the end of the night, she walked away with a Grammy for Best Short Form Music Video for her work on "Lose Con-

Everyone has a birthplace, and so does hip-hop. In hip-hop's case, it was the Bronx in New York City. The sounds of hip-hop helped bring joy and a sense of pride to residents of housing projects such as these.

trol." The "Lose Control" video beat out the Gorillaz's "Feel Good Inc.," Jamiroquai's "Feels Just Like It Should," Martina McBride's "God's Will," and Sarah McLachlan's "World on Fire." This was Ciara's first Grammy, adding to the list of awards and accomplishments she had already gained in her short career.

Ciara had received an additional Grammy honor that night: she was asked to sing during the televised ceremony. Changing from her long white gown into a thigh-skimming black dress, Ciara performed a duet with Adam Levine from the band Maroon 5 in a tribute to the R&B legend Sly Stone. Together they sang "Everyday People," one of Sly's most famous songs.

The song was appropriate; just a few years prior to the performance, Ciara had been an "everyday person," and she still was, despite her star status. "I'm not a Barbie," she said in an interview with *Rolling Stone*. "Just a regular around-the-way girl. I keep it cool. Keep it real."

She came from a military home, and her difficulties moving frequently from one army base to another helped her discover her desire to express herself through music. Her passion for music and performing, as well as her unrelenting determination, catapulted her into the spotlight. She left behind her Atlanta home to become a recording star, and her dreams became realities in a very short time. For Ciara, fame did not come simply because of luck; she sacrificed a great deal to develop her talent and achieve her goals. "There have been a lot of emotional highpoints," she reflects on her official Web site ciaraworld.com. "I've been living my dream. Everything has been so great—winning a Grammy, having my first single go to No. 1, being named 'Entertainer of the Year' at the Soul Train Awards. It's all made me even more motivated." She is now a famous R&B and hip-hop singer, songwriter, dancer, record producer, and actress, proving that talent and emotional drive have rewards.

The Origins of Rhythm and Blues

Ciara is viewed as both an R&B and hip-hop artist. Rhythm and blues, or R&B, is a **genre** of music created in the 1940s. Originally performed by African American artists, it combines elements of jazz, gospel, and blues music. Jerry Wexler of *Billboard* magazine coined the term "rhythm and blues" in 1947. Before this, the style had been known as "race music," a name that was not considered especially racist at the time. Today, it is almost always called R&B instead of rhythm and blues.

The first rock and roll hits were R&B, while modern R&B is related to pop, hip-hop, and rap music. R&B is similar to rap in the style and the focus on the beat, but instead of rapping, the artist sings. It is common today for rappers to be featured on R&B tracks. The **tempo** of R&B songs can vary between slow, soulful ballads and faster dance tunes. There is a great deal of crossover between hip-hop and R&B, however, with R&B singers like Ciara switching into hip-hop mode for certain songs or parts of songs.

Hip-Hop History

Hip-hop music developed in the United States in the mid-1970s and had become a significant part of modern pop culture by the following decade. Hip-hop music has two parts—rapping (also known as MCing) and production and **scratching** (DJing). Its popularity in the United States can be traced back to the African American and Latino communities of the Bronx, a borough in New York City. In the early 1970s, DJs in the Bronx began to isolate the percussion break (or beat portion) from **funk** and disco songs to create a new sound by playing only the break beat, switching back and forth between two record turntables to keep the music going longer. MCs were responsible for introducing the DJ and keeping the audience excited. MCs gradually started to speak more between songs and then over the beat, encouraging people to dance. Their words became more stylized and rhythmic, and the result was a radical new music style called rapping.

Rapping sometimes became a competition, either seriously or in fun, with MCs battling to out-rap each other. MCs would freestyle rap, making up rhymes and lyrics on the spot, usually dissing each other. Whoever got the best response from the audience won the battle.

Hip-hop and the music it influenced didn't stay in New York City, or even on the East and West coasts. It found its way to Atlanta, Georgia, where a young girl was growing—Ciara.

Sometimes the MCs would even leave the DJs behind, creating the beats with only their voices. This technique, called beat boxing, was popular for a while during the early 1980s, but was almost unheard of after that for over a decade. In the early 2000s, however, some artists began to bring back beat boxing and use it in their songs.

Hip-hop is not only a musical genre; it's an entire **culture**. Dance styles, like break dancing and popping, developed along with the music, as people spun and twisted their bodies to the beat. Graffiti artists offered a visual interpretation of the same culture. Fashions developed around what popular hip-hop artists wore. Hip-hop culture has also had a significant impact on language and other aspects of society in the United States and abroad. By the early twenty-first century, hip-hop had become one of the best-selling music genres in the world, and elements of hip-hop culture could be found everywhere.

Despite its popularity, hip-hop artists have often been criticized for endorsing drug use and misogyny (the hatred of women), and for using a great deal of profanity in song lyrics. Some artists argue that their lyrics simply reflect the reality they see on the streets. Others challenge the **stereotypes** about rap and hip-hop artists by using their music to fight against prejudice and injustice. Female artists like Ciara are able to turn the tables and look at situations from a woman's point of view.

Crunk & B Music: R&B for Dancing

Ciara's music combines elements of R&B, hip-hop, and crunk music. Crunk is a form of hip-hop known for its fast, heavy beat, and simple repetitive lyrics. Instead of dealing with social injustice, political opinions, or the life of gangsters, the sole purpose of crunk music is to energize people and get them moving in the clubs. Crunk originated in Memphis, Tennessee, in the late 1980s, but it did not become **mainstream** until the early 2000s. Lil Jon, one of crunk's pioneers, calls it "a state of heightened excitement." He is largely responsible for the popularity of crunk music, since he tailored the heavy bass beats to have a lighter sound appropriate for dance clubs.

Crunk & B is crunk music with a little R&B thrown in. Lil Jon worked with Ciara and Usher to create the new genre. In 2004, Ciara became the first female artist to release a Crunk & B single, "Goodies." Usher was the first male artist to release a single of this genre with "Yeah." Both of these songs were widely popular and hit #1 on the *Billboard* charts. Lil Jon explained to Artist Direct,

> *"Crunk & B songs are R&B songs that get you crunk. They make you wanna wild out. ['Goodies'] is a female empowerment record. The female has the power. The female is in control on this song. This is one of those records for the ladies."*

Ciara's unique style is reflected by her nicknames. She has been called the Princess, Ci Ci, and the Princess of Crunk & B. Lil Jon dubbed her "The First Lady of Crunk & B." Ciara, however, insists that her sound is more R&B pop and that "Goodies" was her only Crunk & B song. Whatever her nickname and whichever genre she records in, Ciara has proven that dreams can come true.

As a "military brat," Ciara spent much of her childhood moving from base to base, city to city. This made it hard to make friends, so Ciara turned to music. Millions of fans are glad she did.

A Little Girl With a Big Dream

Ciara Princess Harris was born on October 25, 1985, in Austin, Texas. Because her parents, Carlton and Jackie Harris, were in the military—her mother in the air force and her father in the army—the family had to move whenever her parents' jobs called for it. As a result, Ciara (pronounced "Sierra") moved a lot during her childhood. She lived on army bases in Germany, New York, California, Arizona, and Nevada. As soon as she started to make friends, she would have to move again, leaving them behind.

Because she did not have many friends, she often had to entertain herself. It was this isolation that made her realize her love of music and songwriting when she was very young. After years of moving, the Harris family finally settled in Atlanta, Georgia, when Ciara was in her early teens. She soon considered Atlanta her home and made friends at school, and then began to focus on her personal ambitions. However, her first goal was not to become a singer.

The Dream Begins

Even when she was very young, Ciara's parents knew their daughter would reach whatever goals she set out to achieve. She had the commitment and discipline necessary for success. She also displayed an interest in music throughout her childhood. Her mother remembers that when she picked Ciara up from day care, her young daughter sang every song on the radio. She not only knew the words to the songs, but she also sang them with surprisingly accurate *pitch*. Ciara had a gift for music and a need to perform. As she matured, her passion for music only increased.

Still, what Ciara really wanted to do was become a model, not a singer. Not until one day, when she was fourteen, did she realize what she wanted to do. She was watching ABC's *Good Morning America* when Destiny's Child began performing live. The group, led by Beyoncé Knowles, looked as though they were having the time of their life as they sang and danced for the crowd. As she watched them perform, her dreams for the future changed. She told Artist Direct, "That's when I made up my mind: 'Hey, I wanna do this.'"

After that, she gave up other activities in hopes of achieving her dream. "I wrote down on paper that I had a goal to be a professional singer and I wanna be there soon. . . . I had to sacrifice a lotta things and I think that was the key thing to get me there," Ciara said on her official Web site.

"I cut out going to the movies, I cut out hanging with friends, I actually told some of my friends, 'This month we're not gonna hang out or talk on the phone.' I don't have too many friends anyway—less is better for me. I cut out the boyfriend—actually I had my heart bro-

ken so I was really like, 'I'm 'bout to do this. I'm 'bout to be on top.'"

Because of her focus and dedication, Ciara's teenage years were very different from those of most people. Instead of going to parties and spending lots of time with her friends, Ciara practiced singing and dancing so she could achieve her goal. Her commitment to her work and her willingness to set aside fun activities for her ultimate goal displayed maturity beyond

Jazze Pha knows real talent, and he saw it in young Ciara. He signed her to his record label when she was just sixteen. The producer turned out to be her music soul mate.

her years. While average students thought mainly about school and their social life, Ciara's mind was filled with ideas about how she could break into the music business. Her peers lived in the present, but Ciara's eyes were always focused on her future. Fortunately, her relentless work ethic would soon be rewarded.

Stepping Stones

Ciara's determination helped her break into the music business. Not long after deciding to become a performer, she

Mainstream music seemed to lack really good dance music, and that was where Ciara excelled. Her music and live performances brought people to their feet, keeping them dancing song after song.

and two other aspiring singers formed a girl group. They performed in Atlanta, so Ciara was close to home. Although the group recorded a few **demos**, they were not successful, and Ciara decided to leave to strike out on her own after just six months. Performing with the group, however, had given Ciara additional experience singing and dancing in front of an audience.

While with the girl group, Ciara had worked on her songwriting ability as well. She found a manager who got her a publishing deal at Red Zone Entertainment Studio in Atlanta, writing lyrics for other artists when she was only fifteen. She wrote lyrics for the Washington D.C.–born songstress Mya and the famous singer Blu Cantrell, but her main goal was always to hear her own voice singing on the radio—preferably singing her own songs. Explaining how she became involved in songwriting, Ciara said to thabiz.com, "It was just something that came from the heart and mind."

When she was sixteen, she met producer Jazze Pha, whom she considers her "music soul mate." In 2002, after only working with her for five days, he signed her to his Sho' Nuff label. He had immediately recognized Ciara's tremendous potential, both because of her attractive physical appearance and her performing abilities. There was a lack of good dance music on the mainstream music scene, and Pha hoped that Ciara's style and work ethic would help fill that void. Despite her youth, Jazze was impressed by the teenager's self-assurance. Her life and career were moving extremely quickly, but Ciara never hesitated; she followed her intuition and believed that signing to Jazze's label was meant to be. "God really put him in my life for a reason," Ciara says of Jazze Pha on Artist Direct. "Our vibe is incredible."

##

Even though she was working on her developing career, Ciara was still a high school student, with all the responsibilities and activities associated with that. She attended North Clayton High School in suburban Atlanta, where she was a prominent member of the track team, competing in relays, the long jump, and the triple jump. Her strong will and competitive nature helped her in those activities as well. She then changed schools, and became the leader of the cheerleading squad at Riverdale High School. Cheerleading meant Ciara performed in front of crowds, an activity that would later help her on stage.

Despite her growing music career, Ciara also had a well-rounded high school career. She was a track star and cheerleader, and both of those activities helped her perform as a music star. Her classmates voted her "Most Likely to Become Famous."

She was popular at school as well, which prepared her for the attention her quick ascent to fame brought. She modeled for a while, following her first dream, and gained experience in acting natural in front of a camera. However, she decided to stop most of her extracurricular activities so that she could focus on her dream of becoming a singer. In fact, she was voted "Most Likely to Become Famous" in high school. She reflects on her Web site, "I watched my peers around me and they were worried about who's wearing what, going to school, trying to talk to somebody, and I was like, 'I'm trying to be somebody. What can I do to get there as soon as possible?'"

Ciara graduated from Riverdale High School in 2003. The next year, Jazze Pha helped Ciara get a contract with the prestigious LaFace Records executive L.A. Reid.

At the start of her career, Ciara reflected on how she was different from most of her peers and talked about her thoughts to Artist Direct:

> *"Throughout life I've experienced a lot more than the typical 18-year-old has. And being in this industry makes you develop more quickly than a typical child would. You mature faster."*

That maturity helped her keep it real as she experienced fame for the first time. The young singer was witnessing her dreams come true, and it was only a matter of time before she would be in the national spotlight.

Collaboration is an important aspect of hip-hop and Crunk & B. So is a big hit. So, when Ciara needed to jump-start her career, she brought in one of the best, Sean Garrett. It worked. Ciara was on her way to stardom.

A Rapidly Rising Star

A recording contract with a well-known label made Ciara's future look bright. She soon learned, however, that her work was far from done simply because she had accomplished the first part of her goal. She had broken into the music business like she had dreamed, but now she wanted more. She wanted to become an international celebrity whose career would span decades. To accomplish this, she would need the tightest dance moves, the freshest image, and the best *collaborators*. And before she could achieve celebrity status, she would need a hit song that would force people to pay attention to her.

It's Goodies to Be on Top

Ciara started creating a demo, but she had difficulty writing lyrics and composing a melody. She knew she wanted to be a positive role model, to be seen as a strong woman, but she struggled with communicating her vision in a song. There was a great deal of pressure on her to create a hit, because the reaction of the public to her first song could determine how successful she would be as an artist. The experienced producers and executives at the record label knew that Ciara had the potential to be a celebrity, but she needed some help taking the first steps toward stardom. LaFace Records exec L. A. Reid called in Sean Garrett, who had helped Usher write his hit single "Yeah," to

When Lil Jon (right) heard Ciara's demo, he knew that a huge star was about to take off. He was so sure, that he produced the song. And when it debuted, he was proved right—it rocketed to #1 and stayed there for seven weeks.

work with Ciara. The process took several days, with Ciara and Sean even writing verses over the phone. When it was done, the creative pair had written "Goodies," an answer song to Petey Pablo's "Freek-a-Leek," which was filled with sexual *innuendo*. Petey Pablo had proclaimed in his song that he wanted a woman for purely physical reasons. Ciara's response was meant to say that women are human beings and not sex objects, that they control their own bodies. Ironically, Petey Pablo was featured on "Goodies."

When Lil Jon heard the demo, he knew it was going to be a huge success. He produced the track, and LaFace released it as a single in the summer of 2004. Audiences loved Ciara's simple message, breathy voice, and sexy image. The song held the #1 position on the *Billboard* Top 100 in the United States for seven weeks, and it made impressive gains on the charts in Australia, Germany, Sweden, and New Zealand. In November of 2004, "Goodies" was certified gold, meaning it had sold 500,000 copies, and it was certified platinum the following January, having sold a million copies. "Goodies" also reached #1 in the United Kingdom in January of 2005.

In the song, Ciara rejects a man's sexual advances, saying she won't give in to him just because he is rich and handsome. "If you're looking for the goodies keep on looking 'cause they stay in the jar," the refrain warns men. "I'm so happy I wrote 'Goodies,'" said Ciara on Artist Direct. "I pray everybody gets it the way they're supposed to." Talking about "Goodies" as a female empowerment song, Ciara commented,

> *"I think we all run across this problem. A guy thinks you're gonna be with him because he's got the iced out chain, he's popular and all that. But that ain't it. That ain't gonna make me give you my number and that's definitely not gonna make me go home with you. It's the truth."*

She added, "I'm kind of putting it down like a guy would. This time it's in my control: 'This is what I want you to do.'"

The music video for "Goodies," directed by Benny Boom, took twenty-seven hours straight to shoot, and also featured Ciara's little sister, Maisy. In the video, Ciara wears a revealing black shirt and dances with a bare midriff, but women are not shown as mere sex objects. Rather, the video follows the message of the song, saying that women should be independent and in charge of their lives. Ciara exudes confidence as she dances, showing she can be sexy without being **submissive**. Besides showing her talent as a singer, the video also helped her earn a reputation as a talented dancer.

First Album

By the time LaFace and Jive Records released Ciara's debut album, *Goodies*, in the United States on September 28, 2004, the singer already had an excited fan base. With the help of Jazze Pha, Sean Garrett, and Lil Jon, the album entered the *Billboard* 200 chart at #3. By November 2004, the album was certified platinum. Ciara became so popular that some clubs reportedly banned Ciara's music for safety reasons; the crowds grew too wild when they heard her infectious dance songs.

Goodies produced three hit singles: "Goodies," "1, 2 Step" featuring Missy Elliott, and "Oh" featuring Ludacris. On April 11, 2005, "1, 2 Step" was released in the United Kingdom. The song reached #3 on the UK charts the first week song downloads were included in determining the singles chart rankings. Had downloads not been included, the song would have only reached the #4 spot, proving just how many of Ciara's fans buy her music online. Ciara's popularity depends a great deal on her young, computer-savvy fans who use the Internet to access her image and music. Ciara had predicted that "1, 2 Step" would be popular: "Some people at the label felt stronger about another record, but I always knew '1, 2 Step' was the second single," she remarked on thabiz.com. "We had to go in and fix it and then it was like, this is the record, hands down." Her instinct proved true: In April 2005, "1, 2 Step" was certified platinum, and "Goodies" was certified multi-platinum.

A fourth single, "And I," a slow love song, peaked at #96 on the charts. It has been speculated that this comparatively poor rating could have been due to the fact that Ciara was already featured on the successful single "Like You" with Bow

Fans were wild about the new female voice on the music scene. They snapped up her recordings and bought tickets to her performances in droves. Ciara had hit the big time—hard.

Wow, and that radio stations did not want to play two Ciara songs at the same time.

In July 2005, Ciara released a DVD called *Goodies: The Videos & More*. The DVD featured music videos, commentaries, and behind-the-scenes footage of her rehearsals for the Soul Train Awards. While her DVD showed fans a little more about Ciara, her collaborative work also earned praise; she had two songs with other artists reach #3 on the *Billboard* Hot 100. Listeners loved her on Missy Elliott's energetic

Soon Ciara was showing up everywhere. She was a regular at award shows and red-carpet events. Fans and the paparazzi couldn't seem to get enough of the young star. Her talents were new, fresh, and hot.

"Lose Control" track, which went on to earn Ciara her first Grammy Award. She also collaborated with Bow Wow (with whom she was romantically involved at the time) on "Like You" and with Field Mob on their single "So What." Her song "Roll With You" was on the soundtrack of the movie *Coach Carter*, and "Get Up," featuring Chamillionaire, was on the *Step Up* soundtrack.

On the Road

"Being on the road, I've met people who tell me that my music inspired them in some way," commented Ciara on her Web site. "When I think about the last few years, I think one of the greatest accomplishments I've had so far is being able to touch people with my music." One way in which she has been able to influence people is to give them a woman's viewpoint in the male-dominated hip-hop world. She was the only female artist on 50 Cent's 2005 *The Massacre* Tour, performing alongside rappers like 50 Cent, Lil Jon, and Ludacris. Since these artists have often been accused of objectifying women, it's ironic that Ciara would tour with them when her first hit single spoke out against such messages. Ciara sang about the power women had over their own bodies, but she was still comfortable performing alongside men whose songs seemed to take away that power. The tour emphasized how different Ciara's message was from the main themes of popular hip-hop.

Ciara continued to perform on tours around the world—with Gwen Stefani, Bow Wow, and Chris Brown, among others—and people loved her music. One of her most important performances was at the 72nd Annual FedEx Orange Bowl in Florida in January of 2006, where she sang at the half-time show. She was nervous to perform in front of the huge stadium audience, knowing she was also facing a tremendously large television audience, but the show went well and her fame increased through the publicity the show gave her.

Being a hip-hop or Crunk & B star isn't all about bling. It's hard work, too. But Ciara wasn't afraid of the hard work, including the rigors of touring. She loves performing in front of her loyal fans.

Influences

As her success increased, many critics began comparing Ciara to Janet Jackson, whom Ciara considers one of her musical idols. Janet's influence on Ciara is evident in many of her music videos; for example, in Ciara's "Get Up" video her outfit, hair, and even makeup are reminiscent of Janet's suggestive style. And just as Janet wears men's clothing in her "I Get Lonely" video, Ciara often wears baggy men's sweat suits in the dance portions of her videos. Some critics consider Ciara the best candidate to fill the dance-pop **niche** long-inhabited by Janet. Ciara admires Janet, saying on her Web site that she has "so much respect for all she's done and whose level of success is something I want to have doing my own thing." Ciara also admires Janet's brother, Michael Jackson, calling him her "ultimate inspiration."

Ciara's other musical influences include Madonna and Whitney Houston, and the late Tupac Shakur's *All Eyez on Me* is her favorite album. These are artists who have faced harsh media coverage and difficult criticism, but who have handled their personal struggles with grace. Ciara told Nick Duerden of *Blender*,

> *"People don't realize just how much pressure being famous brings. Especially when everybody turns on you. Look at the way Whitney, Beyoncé, and Janet have been treated. These are beautiful, humble people who are being persecuted simply because they are famous. And what about Michael, poor, poor Michael?"*

Ciara's musical idols share traits other than personal struggles. Their sound is new and unique, their songs make people want to dance, and their careers have spanned many years. (In Tupac's case, his music has outlasted even his early death.) Ciara wants to reflect these traits in her own career, following in the footsteps of her heroes on her way to fame.

Ciara's fans loved her, and when it was time to cut another CD, they proved it. *Ciara: The Evolution* debuted at #1, quite an achievement for such a young artist. The songs told the story of Ciara's growth in the music industry.

4

Ciara's Evolution

Goodies was fun and simple, but Ciara was ready for something more. "The songs [on *Goodies*] are very catchy," Ciara told Artist Direct. "They're for all demographics, all age ranges. . . . They're not as personal as I want to be. I'd rather be more personal on the second album, once I grow a little more." Her second album, *Ciara: The Evolution*, was released on December 5, 2006, and gave an account of her growth in the music industry and in her personal life after two years in the public eye. "I've learned so much and I feel like I've continued to get better with everything I've done in the last two years," she reflected on her Web site.

"I've been blessed to have friends and family who have been so supportive. I appreciate all that has happened

and now I feel like I'm going to a whole new place with my evolution in fashion, dance, and in my music."

Since she had already established a reputation, many artists and producers wanted to work with her on the album. "What was really cool was that a lot of the producers I wanted to work with felt the same way about working with me," she says on her Web site. Ciara co-wrote and co-produced most of the songs, and her guest producers included Jazze Pha, Rodney Jerkins, Pharrell, Bryan Michael Cox, and will.i.am. Several guest artists also performed on the album, including Lil Jon and 50 Cent. Although there was a lot of guest talent on the album, Ciara remained in control of the songs. "I definitely make sure that I don't have guest features that overshadow me," she said to *Rolling Stone*. "They spice a record; they add a little seasoning to it. I'm the dressing, and they put a little gravy on it."

Before the album's release, from October to December 2006, Ciara went on a seventeen-city club tour to build excitement about *Ciara: The Evolution*. On the tour, she performed songs from her upcoming album, including the singles "Get Up" and "Promise," which had already been released.

Ciara: The Evolution debuted at #1 on the *Billboard* 200 and was soon certified platinum. It sold over 338,000 copies in its first week, 213,000 more than her debut album. Her first single from the album, "Get Up," also featured on the *Step Up* soundtrack, was released in July 2006 and peaked at #7 on the *Billboard* Hot 100. Her second single was "Promise," released in October 2006, and the third was "Like a Boy," released in February 2007. On June 12, 2007, a fourth single, "Can't Leave 'Em Alone" featuring 50 Cent, was released. Album sales were boosted by a bonus DVD included with the CD. The DVD had music videos and over thirty minutes of dance instruction by Ciara so that fans could learn the dance moves she used in "Promise" and "Get Up."

Although the new album included both dance songs and slower ballads, it had a more **retro** feel. Explaining the new sound, Ciara said on her MySpace page,

> *"A lot of the music on this album was inspired by old school records. There was a way music used to feel and I wanted to capture that. . . . All I know is, it feels good with my soul!"*

Evolution might have contained more ballads than her previous release, but Ciara didn't forget the fans who wanted to dance. It also included numbers guaranteed to get people moving, just as Ciara does in her concerts. It's enough to tire out anyone!

Ciara takes her responsibility toward young people very seriously. She wants boys and girls, men and women, to have the same opportunities. These ideas have made her popular with young fans, including those who vote in the Nickelodeon Kid's Choice Awards.

Even so, some critics have dismissed the album as lacking emotion and finesse. They say that true R&B fans do not listen to Ciara because her lyrics do not have deep meaning and the vocals are not strong enough. The record sales, however, have proved that the fans do not agree.

Girl Power

On her second album, Ciara continued her messages of gender equality. Just as "Goodies" told women to resist the sexual advances of men and refuse to be pressured into physical intimacy, "Like a Boy" pointed out the double standard for men and women. While society often accepts, and even applauds, certain things men do in a relationship, such as cheating, women are looked down on if they do the same. In "Like a Boy," Ciara asks, "Would the rules change up or would they still apply if I played you like a toy? Sometimes I wish I could act like a boy." The song challenges the fact that men are told they can cheat on their girlfriends and treat women poorly without any serious consequences. She says in the song that men often come home late and then lie about the reasons. Men, according to Ciara, have a tendency to mistreat the women in their lives and play with their minds. "Like a Boy" points out the injustice of society's attitude and encourages women to stand up for themselves.

Ciara also believes that women should respect themselves by not sleeping around. Unlike some celebrities, Ciara stands out by refusing to be promiscuous. She told *Blender*, "I'm not totally innocent, and I do date. But as a young woman, I also demand respect and I strongly believe . . . in abstinence. Sex before marriage—it's not right." This message in particular challenges an image often associated with hip-hop. Men have dominated the genre since it began in the 1970s, and female singers and rappers have had to struggle to make a name for themselves. It can be difficult for a female musician to perform in a genre where men often boast about objectifying women. Ciara, however, has resisted the demands to sing only suggestive lyrics that portray her as an object instead of as a person. Although she tends to wear form-fitting outfits and clothes that show her midriff, her lyrics oppose the idea that women are only useful when they are pleasing men. Songs such as "Goodies" and "Like a Boy" communicate the message that women and men are equal and should receive the same opportunities, treatment, and respect.

Ciara on the Screen

Ciara is not only a notable figure on the music scene, she has also started to explore her abilities as an actress. In May 2006, Ciara made her acting debut playing Becca Watley in the MTV Films production *All You've Got*. The coming-of-age movie follows the Madonnas and the Phantoms, two rival volleyball teams, as they are forced to cooperate after the Madonnas' school burns down. Ciara enjoyed acting and working with her co-stars: Adrienne Bailon, from 3LW and the Cheetah Girls, and Efren Ramirez. The made-for-TV movie has a positive message, just as Ciara's music does, telling people to set aside their differences and recognize how much we have in common. It is especially geared toward teenage girls, a large part of Ciara's fan base.

In February 2008, Ciara will appear as Amara in the film *Mama, I Want to Sing!* Ciara's character is a preacher's daughter who sings in the church choir before being discovered by James Brown and rising to international pop stardom. The legendary Patti Labelle and Lynn Whitfield also star in this film adaptation of the off-Broadway gospel musical *Mama*. The role is appropriate for Ciara since, like her character, she followed her dreams to become a celebrity in the music world. Ciara hopes that projects like *Mama, I Want to Sing!* will inspire others to pursue their goals and make the most out of their lives.

The music world isn't big enough to hold all of Ciara's talents. In 2006, she began her acting career, and she has plans for even more appearances on the big screen.

It's not all glitz and glamour for Ciara. Though she has to get all dressed up for the increasing number of award shows and premieres she has to attend, she's like most people her age—she loves her jeans.

Awards and Recognitions

Fans around the world can't seem to get enough of Ciara. She was ranked ninth on Yahoo!'s annual list of the most searched-for names on the Internet in December 2005. She has been honored at events such as the American Society of Composers, Authors, and Publishers (ASCAP) Pop Music Awards for songwriting, the 2005 Teen Choice Awards, BET Awards, MTV Music Video Awards, Soul Train Lady of Soul Music Awards, Dirty Awards (for Dirty South hip-hop and crunk), *CosmoGIRL!* magazine Annual Awards, Vibe Awards, and Grammy Awards. Still, she seems to have handled the fame with grace and humility. Before the Grammy Awards, *Rolling Stone* asked her how she would react if she won a Grammy, and she said, "This may sound a little weird to you, but I'm a simple person. My after-Grammy party is me and all my people hanging together, at the hotel. Then I'm gonna celebrate by making more hit records."

At the 19th Annual Soul Train Awards, Ciara was selected to receive the Sammy Davis Jr. Female Entertainer of the Year Award. This honor was particularly impressive because she had earned it after only one year in the major music scene. The popularity of "Goodies" and "1, 2 Step" had quickly propelled her into the spotlight.

Besides her awards and nominations, Ciara has performed in front of huge crowds, both on her own tours and as part of events such as MTV's New Year's Eve special. Such fame has brought opportunities to help others, although it has sometimes led to criticism and vicious rumors as well.

Like many music artists, Ciara does her best to give back to her community and to the world. One of her causes is VH1's Save the Music. In this photo, she is shown performing at one of the benefit concerts.

5

Behind the Pretty Face

Despite the temptations that come with being a celebrity, Ciara does not let her fame go to her head. She told thabiz.com's Dorrie Williams-Wheeler,

> *"You know, I'm pretty much the same person. I take it for what it is. I love the fans. I appreciate it."*

She refuses to let someone else determine her image or control her music. In a 2004 *Rolling Stone* interview she said

> *"Whenever I sing about anything, I think it's important that it's something I can relate to, something I believe in,"*

This is partly why she insists on co-writing and co-producing most of her songs.

Becoming famous so young and so quickly could easily have been overwhelming. Many performers, caught up in their new lifestyle, can too easily become addicted to drugs or binge drinking. Ciara does not want to be one of those people. "I don't drink," she said in an interview with *Rolling Stone*'s Lauren Gitlin before the 2006 Grammy Awards. "I'm not twenty-one, and even when I am, I'm not going to drink. I'm a crazy person, though. I get that natural high." She says that she was raised with a strict sense of morality, and that her religious beliefs contribute to the decisions she makes in her career and in her life. Her avoidance of alcohol and drugs, though, might also be the result of a family member who fell victim to addiction and lost touch with the Harrises.

Ciara wants to use her fame to positively impact people. "I believe I was placed in front of millions of people for a reason," she told *Blender* in May 2005. "People look up to me, they see me as their role model, and that's cool. I've been a role model all my life."

Showing Some Love

Using her celebrity status to help people is important to Ciara. In spite of her hectic schedule, she takes time to help out causes and organizations that are close to her heart. In December 2005, she performed at the Christmas in Washington concert, raising money for the National Children's Hospital. Many of Washington's most influential people attended the concert, including President George W. Bush and the First Lady.

In July of 2006, she performed at the 4th Annual VH1 Save the Music Hamptons Benefit, which raised over $500,000 toward restoring and improving music programs in the public school system. Ciara's songwriting talent, as well as her popularity, inspired the VH1 Save the Music Foundation to choose her to help in their fight for better music education. Ciara is a strong supporter of the educational system, and she believes that it is important for children to be exposed to music at a young age.

Imagine trying to have a relationship with your boyfriend or girlfriend with screaming photographers and paparazzi in your face most of the time. When Ciara dated Bow Wow, they were the subject of a lot of gossip, much of it hurtful. That's a downside of fame.

Okay, Ciara's a music powerhouse and an up-and-coming actress, so what more could she do? The answer, of course, is to become a fashion icon. Ciara has earned a reputation for her sense of style.

Then, in October of the same year, she sang at the This Day Music Festival in Nigeria, alongside people like Snoop Dogg, Busta Rhymes, Beyoncé, and many local artists. The festival celebrated Nigeria's independence and was also meant to help revitalize the local economy and culture.

When Hurricane Katrina struck the Gulf Coast in August of 2005, Ciara wanted to help. Being from Atlanta, the devastation happened nearly in her own backyard. She, along with over forty other celebrities, signed a pool table *Vibe* magazine intended to auction off to help those affected by Katrina. She was also reported to have participated in two different all-star charity singles meant to raise money for the Gulf Coast. One, organized by producer Rodney Jerkins, was to be a cover of the 1979 song "We are Family," while the other, planned by Michael Jackson, was to be called either "I Have This Dream" or "From the Bottom of My Heart," according to various reports. Two years after the hurricane, however, neither of these singles had been released.

The Downside of Fame

Although her career is relatively new, Ciara has had a few struggles with the media. The Internet has helped her build popularity as her fans put up Web sites and discuss her new songs on message boards, but it has also become a vehicle for spreading rumors about her personal life. Speculations that would take days to appear in a tabloid now take only seconds to upload onto the Internet. For example, when Ciara was dating the rapper Bow Wow, word began spreading that the two were engaged after she was noticed wearing a large diamond ring on her left ring finger. Bow Wow, however, insisted that the ring was merely a present.

A year later, in early April 2006, the media reported that Bow Wow had been seen in Los Angeles with another woman. A New York City DJ soon announced that the couple had split up. Many people assumed that Bow Wow was cheating on Ciara, and the constant public scrutiny started to wear on the young starlet's nerves. Representatives from both sides announced that the couple had ended their relationship prior to the incident with the other woman. They insisted that it was an friendly parting and that they wished each other all the best. However nicely the relationship might have ended, Ciara found the constant speculations and questions difficult to handle.

Though that rumor might have been stressful, it was nothing compared to one that had surfaced in 2004, when a rumor developed that Ciara was born a hermaphrodite, meaning that she had both male and female sex organs. Variations on this rumor were that she was transgender, a lesbian, or even a cross-dresser. Many versions of the story said that Ciara had spent her youth with a questionable gender and eventually decided that she wanted to be female. Some people claimed that she had sexual reassignment surgery when she was eleven years old, and that she had discussed the experience with Oprah Winfrey on television. Ciara denies this rumor, saying she's always been female, never had such a surgery, and furthermore, she's never even been on Oprah's television show. Celebrities are often forced to read lies about themselves in the tabloids, and they can either ignore them or go through the trouble of dispelling the rumors. Ciara handles the situation with dignity and laughs off the fact that people are speculating about her sexuality. She told the *New York Daily News*, "You know what's funny? The rumor that I used to be a man." She says that she does not care what others say or think about her, but that it is a shame people spread such lies.

A Passion for Fashion

Ciara is known for her chic, modern fashion sense, whether she is being dubbed "Best Dressed" by critics at the Grammy Awards or is wearing a suggestive outfit in a music video. She cites Gucci, South Pole, and Guess as her favorite fashion labels. The styles of the three companies are very different from each other, which reflects Ciara's unique style. On stage, Ciara tends to wear revealing, tummy-baring outfits, at home she likes to be casual, while at award shows or other celebrity events she often wears simple, elegant dresses. Her style is classy but urban, and regardless of what she wears, her confidence always makes her attractive. Her look and her confidence do not go unnoticed; in May of 2005 she was named one of *Teen People*'s "25 Hottest Stars Under 25."

Along with her music and acting goals, Ciara has another one that is important to her. She wants to start her own fashion line. Few people doubt that she'll be successful when she decides to launch her first collection.

One of Ciara's future goals is to launch her own fashion line, but until that time, she has been keeping busy in the fashion world. In May 2007, Ciara teamed up with Jay-Z to become the new face of his Rocawear line for women. The fashion campaign is entitled "I Will Not Lose," and features images of strong women and stories of women who have overcome difficult situations in life. She is also included, along with pop star Hilary Duff, in an advertisement campaign for the *Candies* clothing and shoe line at Kohl's department store.

Ciara loves to dance—and she's good at it. She also loves to share her gift with others. Her dance agency and instructional DVDs will give everyone the chance to learn her moves!

When she is not rehearsing, performing, or posing at a photo shoot, Ciara loves shopping. "It is so soothing to see those racks of clothes," she said to thabiz.com. "Sometimes the good stuff is far back in the racks. I also like shopping for shoes. I love shoes."

New Projects

On May 11, 2007, Ciara announced that she would host *Glamour* magazine's Reel Music contest during its second year. She chose three emerging female music artists to be a part of the project: Tiffany Evans, Paula Campbell, and Samantha Jade. People could listen to their music online and vote for their favorite contestant. The winner would be showcased in a music video directed by Ciara. This project allows Ciara to explore her interest in directing, as well as her devotion to furthering the careers of other talented music artists.

She's also started her own dance agency, Universal Dance Agency (UDA) in her hometown of Atlanta. She has always enjoyed dancing and teaching other people her dance moves. The dance instruction on her *Goodies: The Videos and More* DVD was only a beginning. She told AOL Music that she hoped her dance agency would "give people that love to dance a chance to do what they want to do—for videos or performances for plays."

Ciara continues to tour. During August and September of 2007, she performed in BET's Scream Tour, Screamfest '07, with rapper T.I., as well as Yung Joc and Lloyd Banks.

The Ride Continues

Throughout her life, Ciara has displayed her tenacity and determination to accomplish her goals. She typically sleeps no more than four hours a night, too busy and driven to relax any longer than that. She looks to the future with hungry eyes, eagerly awaiting new opportunities and experiences. She has achieved her dream of becoming a successful singer, but

It's hard to believe that Ciara has come so far so quickly. But if you listen to her songs, you'll see why. Unlike others who have shot to stardom quickly, only to crash and burn shortly after, there's no sign that Ciara's career won't continue to rise.

she has other goals. She realizes that, to be truly successful in the modern music scene, artists must create an empire and become involved in numerous fields. In the upcoming years, she hopes to start her own record label. She plans on opening a restaurant and breaking into real estate. She also dreams of creating her own clothing line. Her urban chic style has shown audiences everywhere that women can be sexy without being promiscuous or submissive to men. Ciara also plans to expand her film career because she thoroughly enjoys acting and hopes that the positive messages in her movies will both entertain and have an impact on audiences. She will continue to develop her dance agency so that aspiring performers will receive high-quality training.

Even with these new ventures, the dreams from her child-hood remain. Ciara strives to sell millions of records and achieve lasting fame. She doesn't want to be just another singer, famous for a few hits and then forgotten. "It's not just about penning clever lyrics and singing and dancing to a banging track," Ciara told Artist Direct.

"My goal is to deliver a positive message and let people know they're not the only one going through things. . . . I've been blessed to be able to counsel my peers. I'm here to deliver a message, and I think the impression that you make is very important. I don't wanna write records just to write. I wanna have a message to everything that I write. That gives you longevity."

Ciara is certainly on the path to accomplishing her goals. With talent, determination, and a vision as amazing as hers, the little girl who sang along with the radio will be heard on the radio for many years to come.

1940s Rhythm and blues develops.

1970s Hip-hop develops in the Bronx section of New York City.

1980s Crunk originates in Memphis, Tennessee.

Oct. 25, 1985 Ciara is born in Austin, Texas.

2002 Ciara signs with the record label Sho' Nuff.

2003 Ciara graduates from Riverdale High School.

2004 Ciara signs with LaFace Records.

2004 Ciara's first single, "Goodies" is released and hits #1; it is certified gold in November.

2004 Ciara becomes the first female artist to release a Crunk & B single.

Sept. 28, 2004 Ciara's debut album is released; it is certified platinum in November.

2005 Ciara is the only female artist to perform on 50 Cent's *The Massacre* Tour.

April 2005 "1, 2 Step" is certified platinum, and "Goodies" is certified multi-platinum.

July 2005 Ciara releases a DVD, *Goodies: The Videos & More*.

Dec. 2005 Ciara performs at the Christmas in Washington concert.

Dec. 9, 2005 Ciara ranks ninth on Yahoo!'s annual list of the most searched-for names on the Internet.

2006 Ciara wins a Grammy Award and performs at the ceremony.

Jan. 2006 Ciara performs at the half-time show of the Orange Bowl.

May 2006 Ciara makes her acting debut in *All You've Got*.

July 2006 Ciara performs at the 4th Annual VH1 Save the Music Hamptons Benefit.

Oct. 2006 Ciara performs at the This Day Music Festival in Nigeria.

Dec. 5, 2006 Ciara's second album, *Ciara: The Evolution*, debuts at #1.

May 2007 Ciara becomes the new face of Rocawear clothing line.

May 11, 2007 Ciara announces that she will host *Glamour*'s Reel Music contest.

Aug.–Sept. 2007 Ciara tours with BET's Scream Tour, Screamfest '07.

Feb. 2008 Ciara stars in *Mama, I Want to Sing!*

Albums

2004 *Goodies*

2006 *Ciara: The Evolution*

Number-One Singles

2004 "Goodies" (with Petey Pablo)

2006 "Promise"

DVDs

2005 *Goodies: Videos and More*

Awards and Recognition

2005 BET Awards: Best Collaboration (for "1, 2 Step"); *CosmoGIRL!* Magazine Annual Awards: Born to Lead Award; MTV Video Music Awards: Best Dance Video (for "Lose Control" with Missy Elliott and Fatman Scoop), Best Hip-Hop Video (for "Lose Control" with Missy Elliott and Fatman Scoop); Soul Train Lady of Music Awards: Best Dance Cut (for "1, 2 Step"), Best R&B Soul/Rap New Artist (for "1, 2 Step"), Best Video (for "Lose Control" with Missy Elliott and Fatman Scoop); Soul Train Music Awards: Best R&B/Soul or Rap

New Artist, Sammy Davis Jr. Female Entertainer of the Year; *Vibe* Awards: Coolest Collaboration (for "Oh").

2006   ASCAP: Best Performed Songs in the ASCAP Repertory for the 2005 Survey Year (for "Goodies," "1, 2 Step," and Oh); Dirty Awards: Best Dance Video (for "Get Up"); Grammy Awards: Best Short Form Video (for "Lose Control" with Missy Elliott and Fatman Scoop); Soul Train Music Awards: Best Dance Cut (for "Lose Control" with Missy Elliott and Fatman Scoop).

Books

Bogdanov, Vladimir, Chris Woodstra, Steven Thomas Erlewine, and John Bush (eds.). *All Music Guide to Hip-Hop: The Definitive Guide to Rap and Hip-Hop.* San Francisco, Calif.: Backbeat Books, 2003.

Chang, Jeff. *Can't Stop Won't Stop: A History of the Hip-Hop Generation.* New York: Picador, 2005.

George, Nelson. *Hip Hop America.* New York: Penguin, 2005.

Leavitt, Amie. *Ciara.* Hockessin, Del.: Mitchell Lane, 2007.

Light, Alan (ed.). *The Vibe History of Hip Hop.* New York: Three Rivers Press, 1999.

Walker, Ida. *Hip-Hop Around the World.* Broomall, Pa.: Mason Crest, 2008.

Waters, Rosa. *Hip-Hop: A Short History.* Broomall, Pa.: Mason Crest, 2007.

Web Sites

Ciara Official Web Site
www.ciaraworld.com

Ciara on MySpace
www.myspace.com/ciara

Glossary

collaborators—Individuals who work together to create a project.

culture—The beliefs, customs, practices, and social behavior of a particular nation or people.

demos—Recorded samples of music produced for promotional purposes.

funk—A type of popular music that comes from jazz, blues, and soul and is characterized by a heavy rhythmic bass.

genre—A category into which an artistic work can be placed based on its form, style, or subject matter.

innuendo—An indirect remark that usually carries a suggestion of something improper.

mainstream—The ideas, actions, and values that are most widely accepted by a group or society.

niche—A position or activity that suits someone's talents and personality.

pitch—The level of a sound in the scale.

retro—Modeled on something from the past.

scratching—Purposely dragging the record needle across a playing record.

stereotypes—Oversimplified images or ideas, often based on incomplete or inaccurate information, held by one person or group about another.

submissive—Tending to give in to the demands or authority of others.

tempo—The speed at which a musical composition is played.

Index

About the Author

Jacquelyn Simone is continuing her education in upstate New York, where she is pursuing a degree in journalism. She has always been fascinated by different musical genres and enjoys singing and playing guitar as well as listening to music.

Picture Credits

Akasha Multimedia / PR Photos: pp. 44, 48
Bielawski, Adam / PR Photos: front cover, pp. 2, 16, 29, 32, 37, 52
Gabber, David / PR Photos: pp. 22, 38, 54
Harris, Glenn / PR Photos: p. 41
Hatcher, Chris / PR Photos: pp. 8, 47
iStockphoto:
    Dawson, Andrew: p. 10
    Eckert, Gabriel: p. 13
Kirkland, Dean / PR Photos: pp. 19, 26
Legato, Scott / PR Photos: p. 20
Mayer, Janet / PR Photos: pp. 34, 42
Thompson, Terry / PR Photos: p. 30
Walck, Tom / PR Photos: p. 24
Wild1 / PR Photos: p. 51